SUMMARY
OF

THE RUSSIA HOAX:

THE ILLICIT SCHEME TO CLEAR HILLARY CLINTON AND FRAME DONALD TRUMP

By

GREGG JARRETT

Brought to you by Book HOUSE

Table of Contents

EXECUTIVE SUMMARY

The book sterns to reveal the damage wrought when those in power tend to abuse it. It is an intertwined set of stories about government officials and how they abused their offices and violated/misused the law to suit their ill motives. Notable amongst others are Hillary Clinton and James Comey and also Donald Trump who became a victim of abuse of power as he faced multiple challenges as most Government officials sought to ruin his presidential campaign and even his administration.

CHAPTER 1: HILLARY CLINTON'S EMAIL SERVER

Here in the administration of Hillary Clinton, corruption was the order of the day. while serving as the secretary of state operated a private email server in the basement of her home, by which she sent an received highly classified information's of the government which was contrary to the rules required by the state department, and also the limitation placed by the Freedom Of Information Act(FOIA).This act of Clinton which threatened National security was questionable upon discovery, her excuses were baseless and therefore could not hold water. Her action ordinarily amounted to a criminal prosecution also the act of covering up her tracks like wiping of some mails in spite of an order to preserve it by the congress added up to her criminal charges. Howbeit, she seemed to have her way around the government and therefore escaped indictment.

CHAPTER 2: COMEY CONTORTS THE LAW TO CLEAR CLINTON

Having spent a year gathering of incriminating evidence of wrongdoing against Clinton, FBI director James Comey in his interview, gave a detailed evidence of crime but to the astonishment of all, didn't refer Clinton for prosecution. Comey laid a meticulous case of how Clinton broke the law which reasonably sufficed for criminal prosecution to present a statement of how Clinton broke the law, how classified emails were found on her private server in her residence without any approval and also did not stop there but went ahead to the media. Comey but then turned to offer an implausible reason why she should not be prosecuted on the basis that, it was more of speculation on his side and the law does not accept this as a valid basis and hence no prosecutor will bring such a case. Moreover, any other prosecutor would have brought such a case of which any have done so under similar circumstances. It was revealed that Comey's decision not to prosecute was preconceived action Vexed the entire populace, Other FBI agents held that it was wrong in fact a violation of the FBI standards. Why Comey Usurped the authority of the Attorney General and also reached conclusions even before the fact-finding process was concluded, suggested basis which resulted in obstruction of Justice. Facts later emerged that suggested that the investigation was corrupted from several persons within the FBI and the Justice Department.

CHAPTER 3:"THE FIX"

Questions arose as to why Comey absolved Clinton from prosecution. It remained puzzling, suspicious and counter intuitive to the law. Troubling questions persisted over time and several names began to emerge. All of which were FBI officials who were instrumental in the handling of the Clinton's case. Notable amongst all, was two FBI agents Peter Strzok and his lover Lisa page who were believed to have corrupted the investigative process of Clinton's case. Their text messages to each other was discovered which revealed hostility toward Trump and adoring compliments about Clinton that is to say, bias already existed while they carried on investigation.

The text also revealed their awareness of the decision of not prosecuting Clinton. It there makes sense to say that comey's decision was predetermined. Peter Strzok was also suspected of editing the statement of Comey, thereby removing certain critical wordings which would have sufficed for a finding of criminality. It became obvious that the FBI was flawed with corruption whilst carryon the investigation of Clinton's.

CHAPTER 4: "CLINTON'S GREED AND URANUIM ONE"

There is no greater disaster than greed... The way of Lao Tzu, Ancient Chinese Philosopher. Man's desires are insatiable. Can never be satisfied, his appetite keeps increasing with time, there is never a place of satisfaction, man wants to keep climbing the ladder of success.

This chapter is introduced with an elucidation of the source of the Clinton's wealth, contrary to what Hillary Clinton had told America and the world about their financial status when her husband left office how they were not only broke but in debt. But they grew to riches again through Bill Clinton's speaking arrangement in foreign countries and Hillary's job as Secretary of state. Bill according to a

2014 analysis *The Washington post* determined that Bill was paid roughly $105 million for speeches he made at different events

The Clinton Foundation

At the end of the Bill Clinton presidency, the couple established a non-profit organization named the **Clinton Foundation,** a lot of money was pumped into the foundation by international corporations and individuals with an interior motive of gaining favour with the Clintons to advance their personal interest. Before Hillary was confirmed secretary of state, she promised transparency in the donation of funds into the foundation and there will be no conflict of interest between her position as Secretary of State and the foundation. She did not follow through with her promise, it was discovered that several donations from seven foreign

countries were not accounted for as promised.
As discovered by **The Hill**.

Victor David Hanson, a historian at the
Hoover Institution at Stanford University
accused the Clintons of peddling both access
and influence in what he characterized as a
shameless scheme driven by inordinate greed.
Many of the largest contributions to the
Clinton Foundation were made by people and
Shell companies connected to a Russian-
controlled business called Uranium One,
which managed through a series of clever
manuevers, to seize control of a sizable
percentage of America prized uranium assets.
Russia through Uranium One gained a hold of
arguably 20% of the uranium assets in the
United States. Frank Giustra, Ian Telfer are
names that are obviously linked with the
scandal of the donations made to the Clinton
Foundation as a means to gain influence in

America policy decision making. The Clintons denied all the allegations against the foundation and maintained that all donations were in no way connected to any influence in the policies of the United States.

The Clinton's were adept at hiding evidence as no direct trace or evidence has been recovered from all investigations carried out on the Clinton Foundation or Hillary Clinton to determine their connections with Russia and influencing America Uranium policies to favour Russia. But the timing of contributions and sheer volume of Clintons enrichment strongly suggest something more than a coincidence. The Nuclear Regulatory Commission assured Congress that even if Russia owned 20% of the uranium assets it could not export it to Russia. The Russians have cleverly through Canada exported uranium yellowcake to Iran. The Yellowcake is a concentrated uranium power that can be enriched and processed for nuclear weapons. New York Times, published a front-page headline of the Clinton Foundation/Russia scandal titled "Cash Flowed to the Clinton Foundation Amid Russian Uranium Deal". An informant William Douglas Campbell allegedly witnessed conversations about how "Russian nuclear officials tried to ingratiate themselves with the Clintons. Documents also showed connections of millions of dollars from Russia's nuclear industry to an American entity that had provided assistance to Bill Clinton's foundation. Robert Mueller, James Comey and Rod Rosenstein were consecutive FBI directors during all the periods of the investigations of this quid pro quo conspiracy and collusion between the Clintons and Russia, but they never brought forward any findings to support this alleged theory of conspiracy. Douglas Band is another key to unravel this mystery. Huma Abedin is also entangled in this, he is a long-time friend of Hillary and held three Jobs simultaneously; deputy chief of staff to the secretary of state, a paid consultant to the Clinton Foundation, and an income-earning consultant in Band's company Teneo. Once the Clintons were out of office and what they had could not influence directly the policies of the United States, it was observed that Bill Clinton's speech pay checks that used to be in millions of dollars fell as low as $300,000. The Clinton Foundation experienced setback in terms of donations it received as well.

CHAPTER 5: THE FRAUDULENT CASE AGAINST DONALD TRUMP

The FBI launched an investigation on Donald Trump without a probable cause. Just when they had exonerated Clinton of an indictment, they turned their attention to the only person who could halt her march to the white house. The FBI secretly began an investigation of whether the Russian Government attempted to interfere with the presidential election. Yes, the Russian president Vladimir Putin held a grudge against Clinton and had preference for Trump, there was no evidence of collusion between the Russia and Trump. Not a single shred of evidence was produced. Also there existed recognisable bias by the FBI agent who led the investigation Peter Strzok over Trump.

At the time the investigation was launched, there was no legitimate basis for doing so. This was in itself a violation of the guidelines of Attorney General with which the operations of the FBI were bound. The investigation soon went public and the key term used by everyone was "collusion" yet it was revealed that the term "collusion" was not a crime under any of the American laws. Despite the allegation of collusion by various top officials, there existed not a whiff of evidence, it appeared to have been smoked without fire. Also talking to Russians was not a crime, America had freedom of association with any one Russian inclusive. The only Reason the FBI gave to support their investigation could not hold water as it was based on wide speculations and gossips.

CHAPTER 6: THE FABRICATED "DOSSIER" USED AGAINST TRUMP –

The Central Intelligence Agency of the United States is known for its secrecy in carrying on its functions to defend the State from attacks. John Brennan of the CIA during Obama's administration brought up some intelligence information about a "dossier" alleging presidential candidate Donald Trump of collusion with Russia, he alerted the FBI who opened its Trump-Russia investigation. The dossier contained information's of how Russia helped presidential candidate Donald Trump win the election. In its entirety the document contained no direct information or pressing evidence, as it was majorly records of hearsay evidence which were not incapable of being verified and thus incredible. The "dossier" was actually a compendium of seventeen consecutive memos believed to be penned by Christopher Steele former British spy between June and December 2016. He was discovered to have had no direct access to information's he gave in the dossier, however Brennan adopted the information. And being a Clinton loyalist set out to use it against Donald Trump. Stephen Cohen, professor of Russia studies at the New York University debunked information's Brennan published as unrealistic and lacked real proofs. Any intelligent person would have quickly dismissed the content of the "dossier" as nothing more than a collection of unsubstantiated assertions to smear Trump. Newsweek turned a critical eye to the "dossier" and published a story "Thirteen Things That Don't Add up in the Russia-Trump Intelligence Dossier". The "dossier" alleged Trumps attorney Michael Cohen, secretly met with Russians in August 2016 to arrange cash payment, while records showed contrary. Russian President Vladimar Putin offered that the "dossier" was an attempt by the outgoing American president Barack Obama to "undermine the legitimacy of the president elect" Carter Page was a member of the Trump campaign team and was linked severally with the Russians and assumed to have made deals with them on behalf of Donald Trump, he defended all the allegations and cleared himself.

CHAPTER 7: GOVERNMENT ABUSE OF SURVEILLANCE

Usually, for the Government to begin an investigation on someone, there must exist a probable cause for it. This means that there must be a fair probability that the surveillance will produce evidence of a crime. An infamous Dossier was produced as evidence of trump's collaboration with Russia. The Dossier was not a 100% reliable but it seemed that they were more interested in the political havoc that can be brought through the dossier than the truth. Also, the FBI and DOJ knew the Dossier was unverified, they knew it was paid for by Clinton, they also knew if the bias harboured by Steele who complied it and his hatred for Trump. But in spite of the odds, the FBI and DOJ used it anyway. Many other facts revealed the violation of various laws just to pin Trump to a crime he didn't commit. An unverified Report to discredit a political opponent in a presidential campaign is about as egregious as one could imagine.

CHAPTER 8: MEETING WITH RUSSIANS IS NOT A CRIME-

The American Constitution in its first amendment, gives Americans the freedom of association with whom ever they want and places no limitation on the Russians. Howbeit, there have been this false mentality that the Russians are threats to national security, so that it became normatively wrong to speak to the Russians. An illustration of this fact was the duty placed on Donald Trump's son to notify the FBI of a meeting he had with a Russian lawyer at Trump Tower during the presidential campaign. The meeting between Trump Jr and the Russian lawyer, was considered "collusion" with the Russians and tainted with all manner of illegality. Renown scholars branded it as treason. This was surprising as all allegations had little or no support of law. Meeting with a Russian lawyer or receiving of information from him was treason by any stretch of the imagination.

CHAPTER 9: FLYNN'S FIRING, SESSIONS RECUSAL AND THE CANNING OF COMEY

Upon assuming the office of president, Donald Trump appointed General Michael Flynn to serve as National Security Adviser and Senator Jeff Sessions as Attorney General. This proved unwise as a mistake by them haunted his first year in office and beyond. Flynn did not last a month in his office as he was fired for dishonesty about his conversation with the Russian Ambassador Kislyak.Despite his faulty memory about his discussion with Kislyak,he did nothing wrong. Jeff Sessions challenge on the other hand ensued from omission of facts other than commission of any crime. Jeff sessions recused himself from the investigation of the Trump Russia collusion. This was a grievous mistake by Sessions. It appeared that he had planned the recusal even before coming into office. Then there was Comey, Director of FBI. Comey had violated a lot of regulations in him handling Clintons email case and was justifiably fired by Trump. However, the public didn't see it this way as they assumed it was a way of ruining the ongoing Trump Russia probe. All these series of events created a political upheaval that threatened jeopardize Trumps presidency.

Donald Trump did not have much experience in elected public office and so ought to have leaned on those with experience but instead he made decisions against the advice of people like Obama that ended up being a regrettable mistake. He appointed General Michael Flynn and Senator Jeff Sessions as National Security

Adviser and Attorney General respectively. Howbeit he never envisaged that this decision would haunt his first year in office and beyond.

Flynn did not last up to a month in his office as he was fired for being less than honest with the vice president about his conversation with the Russia AmbassadorSergey Kislyak.It wouldn't even be totally correct to say Flynn had lied about his conversation because he wasn't reasonably expected to repeat every single word of the conversation with Kislyak. And apart from his faulty memory about his discussion with the Russian ambassador, He did nothing wrong. There was no evidence of any crime committed by him. Jeff Session's challenge on the other hand ensued from an omission of fact other than the commission of any wrongful act, which fact was about an imprudent recusal that would prove fateful to

Trump. Barely three weeks into his office, he recused himself from anything that had to do with the Trump Russia probe. This was a grievous mistake but it appeared that he had planned the recusal even before he was appointed. Then there was James Comey, Director of the FBI. Comey had violated the law severally whilst he handled Clinton's email case and was justifiably fired by the President Trump. Upon his departure however, he absconded with government classified documents and leaked them to the media which precipitated the appointment of Robert Mueller as Special Counsel to investigate the president. These series of events created a political upheaval that threaten to jeopardize Trumps presidency as the events were flash points for specious claims that Trump not only colluded with Russians but attempted to obstruct justice. Flynn continuously held that he did no wrong but eventually, he agreed to plead guilty.

It was discovered that he took the plea because the ruthless prosecutor left him no choice as pleading otherwise would drive him into financial ruin and also leave his son at the risk of being probed. Had he continued to stand on his ground, there was a slim possibility of him being convicted from that case. All of his acts were in the normal cause of carrying out his duties an NSA. He did not violate any codified crime. As for Comey, he should have been fired the day he declared his decision to absolve Clinton of prosecution. He defied several laws also destroyed the public's trust in the FBI. Comey's lack of integrity and defiance of rules and regulation was what brought his downfall and not grudge or ill motives if Trump. Comey was fired fir reasons that was entirely justified howbeit, it created demands that for the impeachment of President Trump, but their claims against Trump in truth and in law were erroneous hence it was a tussle that Trump scaled through.

CHAPTER 10:

"OBSTRUCTION OF

JUSTICE"

Men are more often bribed by their loyalties
and ambitions than by money" Justice Robert
H. Jackson, United States V. Wunderlich, 342
U.S 98 (1951) There is nothing wrong with
ambition. But ambition without character or
principles is what turns good men into bad
men. They well know right from wrong, but
are too willing to hide the truth in favour of
advancing their own designs. Their loyalty is
to themselves. James Comey, an ex FBI
director decides to leak dirt on president
Donald Trump after he was sacked. He leaked
information alleging obstruction of justice by
the president in the Michael Flynn's case.
Michael Flynn was former national security
adviser to the president, who at the time was a

suspect being investigated by the FBI. Comey didn't want to leak the information himself, he employed the assistance of a law professor Daniel Richman of Columbia Law School to leak the information in a tome he titled 'A Higher Loyalty: Truth, Lies, And Leadership' with the objective that it would trigger the appointment of a special counsel to investigate the man who had just fired him. Obstruction of justice is defined in a series of statuses, the most relevant of which is 18 U.S.C 1505: "Whoever corruptly... influences, obstructs, or impedes or endeavours to influence, obstruct, or impede the due and proper administration of the law under which any pending proceeding is being had before any department or agency of the United States... shall be fined under this title, imprisoned not more than 5 years, or both." While the term 'corruptly' as it applies to the obstruction of justice statute according to

Arthur Andersen V. United States was defined as "wrongful, immoral, depraved, or evil" and for this statute to be applied it requires proof of consciousness of the accused. For years James Comey carefully cultivated a public portrait of himself as a grown-up Boy Scout, honest and morally straight. The records show that he was less than honest, engaged in acts of questionably legality, and abused his power to further his ambitions. During an interrogation with the Senate Judicial Committee he confessed that he deliberately leaked to "a friend" the contents of the presidential memorandums memorializing his conversations with Trump. It was a devious scheme, which he knew the media would be willing to trash Trump by contorting the memos' contents and misconstruing the law to accuse the president of obstruction of justice. The information Comey leaked were properties of the United States and he had no right to take them when he left office. The act of concealing information and waiting till he left office before presenting It to public was another dent in his character and brought questions as to the authenticity of whatever he said and this act are criminal in nature. Far from the image of an honest man which James Comey puts up, he sought to mislead, deflect and deceive. And his accusations of obstruction of justice falls back on him. His plan to covert presidential memos for his own use, then leak them to the media to damage Trump suggests a willingness to defy rules, regulations and federal laws with impunity.

CHAPTER 11: THE ILLEGITIMATE APPOINTMENT OF ROBERT MUELLER-

Upholding justice is now a secondary pursuit for Government officials. Prosecutors have been carried away with other things such as politics and material satisfaction. The appiontment of Robert Mueller to the office of the special counsel was an illustration of this. The regulations governing the selection were misused. Rossenstein who appointed Mueller didn't comply with the rules relating to the appointment of a special counsel.

His appointment also exceeded the intended limits of a special counsel. Again, the conflicts of interest of both Mueller and Rossenstein was so acute that it suggested an undisputable bias and thus the law required them to recuse themselves from the investigation of Trump, however it appeared that they were more concerned with damaging Trumps tenure than seeing to it that justice and fairness is upheld.

Mueller forged ahead despite the legal obstacles but continued to violate various special counsel regulations. Facts were revealed that clearly showed that Rossenstein and Mueller circumvented the law to pursue their interest.

Again, the way Mueller organised his investigation against Trump showed heavy bias, for instance he appointed political partisans all of which had ties or allegiance with democrats, Obama or Clinton to investigate Trump. It was obvious that the special counsel team was more concerned with the damage that could be done to the presidency than the search for justice and fairness. It seemed that the law and public offices of government became a tool used to plot evil.

Made in the USA
Middletown, DE
31 August 2018